Vickers Supermarine Spitfire IX

Robert Grudzień

Introduction

In September 1941 Royal Air Force pilots reported the presence of a new superb German fighter with radial engine. It was the Focke-Wulf FW190A which outclassed the British Spitfire V in the dive, climb and rate of roll, and was about 30 mph faster. This new threat called the "Butcher Bird" created an urgent need to produce a fighter equal to as FW190A was.

The intended successor of the Spitfire V, the improved Spitfire VIII with a strengthened fuselage, retractable tail wheel, fuel tanks in wing leading edges and the Merlin 61 engine was, unfortunately, still not ready for production due to necessary modifications of the tooling. Therefore, based on successful test results of a Spitfire III airframe with the Merlin 60, the Air Ministry decided to order a conversion of the Spitfire V with the powerful Merlin 61 engine, as the fastest solution. The new variant of the Supermarine fighter was designated the Spitfire IX (or Supermarine type 361 and type 378, the latter in the tropicalised version). The modifications were limited to a minimum: the longer and heavier power unit required reinforcement of the longerons and extended cowlings, the oil cooler and the newly added intercooler were located in two similar fairings under wings, each combined with a half of the engine radiator. A four bladed 10ft 9in propeller was installed. The universal armament wing (similar to the C wing of the Spitfire V, although never called as such in the Mk IX!) with two 20mm cannon and four 0.303in machine guns was used as standard at the first stage. Later, 20mm cannon and two 0.5in machine guns were installed in the wing, and this armament was known as the "(e) wing". There were further visible modifications like the broad chord rudder, the pointed wing tips for improved high altitude performance and clipped ones for better rate of roll. Subsequently Spitfire IXs– were equipped with a large filter on the carburettor air intake.

- Spitfire IX was used in variety of roles and there were the following main versions:
- Spitfire F.IX with Merlin 61 and Merlin 63 engines
- Spitfire LF.IX with Merlin 66 engine optimised for low altitude performance
- Spitfire HF.IX with Merlin 70 engine optimised for high altitude performance
- Spitfire FR.IX – fighter reconnaissance version (none built as such, all converted from fighter aircraft)
- Spitfire T.9 – training, two-seater version (none built as such, all converted from single-seat fighter aircraft)

A total of 5663 Spitfire IXs were built in all versions.

Acknowledgement

I wish to thank Wojtek Matusiak for his invaluable support during creation of the book. Additionaly I am grateful for help of Steven McLean and Wojciech Łuczak.

1

Spitfire N3297 Boscombe Down, winter 1941–1942.

Built as a prototype of the Spitfire III first flown by Jeffrey Quill on 16 March 1940. In September 1941, rebuilt with a new Merlin 61, it became the first Spitfire IX prototype. The A-wing, retractable tail wheel and flat-sided canopy attract attention. The original engine cowling panels were used, but were extended, and bulged fairings were added over the intercooler. The airframe was already heavily worn by then, but still retained Dark Green and Dark Earth top surfaces and Yellow undersides. Original factory-applied serial number. The spinner of the four-blade propeller was in Sky. Type "A" roundels and fin flash. The bottom of the fuselage from the carburetor air intake to mid-fuselage behind the wing was probably painted black.

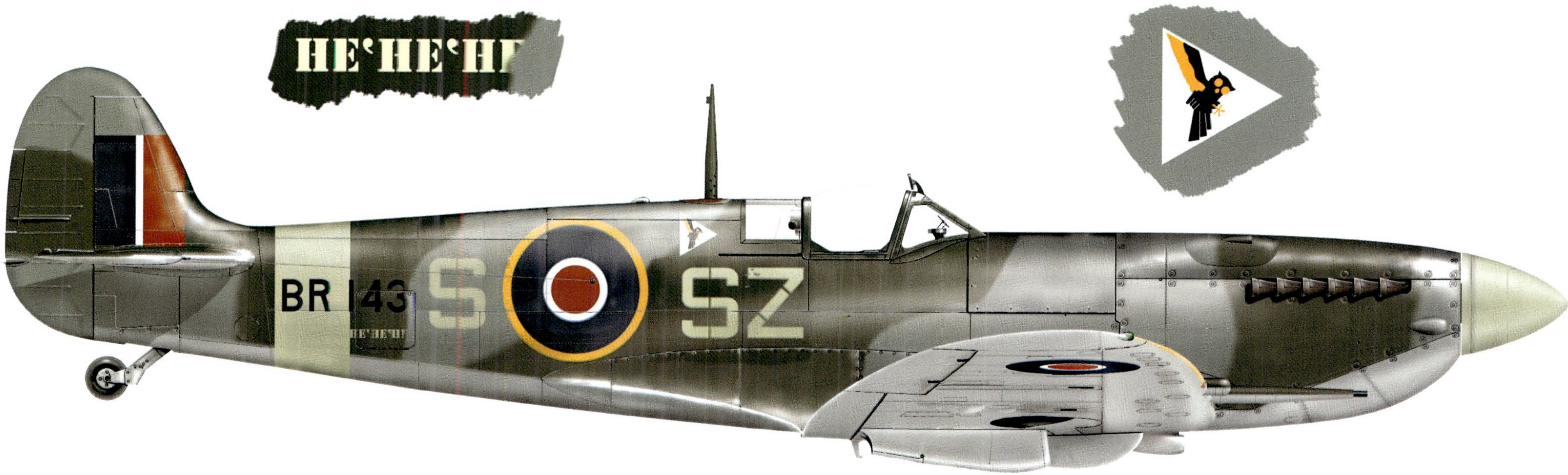

Spitfire F.IX BR143 SZ●S, No. 316 Squadron Polish AF, Northolt, Spring 1943.

Built as a Spitfire V then converted to an F.IX with a Rolls-Royce Merlin 61 engine. Very early style engine cowlings – extended panels from a Spitfire V with bulged fairings over the intercooler. Early style air scoop on the starboard side of top cowling. Similar modified lower cowl with external battery access door. The tear-drop fairing on the starboard cowling just aft of the propeller was typical for aircraft with Merlin 61 engine. Note the 30 gal. drop tank under the fuselage. IFF antenna wire is visible between the tailplane and the fuselage inlet on the roundel. Standard Day Fighter camouflage of Dark Green and Ocean Grey on the upper surfaces and Medium Sea Grey on the lower. The spinner and the 18 inch fuselage band in Sky. Yellow stripe along the leading edge of the wing. The badge of No. 316 Squadron aft of the cockpit. Under the SZ stencils stains of paint used to cover the previous UZ squadron code can be visible. Note partially painted over inscription „HE'HE'HE" most probably left by the previous marking of the squadron.

3

Spitfire F.IX BS342 R, No. 238 Squadron RAF, Italy 1943.

Another Spitfire originally built as a Mk V and converted to Mk IX immediately at Rolls-Royce Hucknall. It shows the engine cowling characteristic for this modification. Other changes are interesting: pointed (high altitude) wingtips, no antenna mast, no rear-view mirror, and no outer cannon fairings. These modifications may have been made to improve performance. Another modification is the Aboukir filter on the carburetor air intake, rarely seen on the Spitfire IX. Camouflage: Day Fighter High Flying – Medium Sea Grey on the upper surfaces and PRU Blue underneath. Two-tone roundel on the fuselage, but a three-tone fin flash, not correct with this scheme. Small (circa 5") black serial number. The port engine cowling displays a painting of Hydra, the emblem of No. 238 Squadron.

Spitfire F.IX BR592 SH●N, No. 64 Squadron RAF, Summer 1942.

One of the first Supermarine-built Spitfire in the F.IX version. A top engine cowling with small bulged fairings similar to the Spitfire V, an early rectangular rear-view mirror, and a flat-sided canopy are the hallmarks of the first batch of Spitfire IXs from this factory. Standard Day Fighter scheme of Dark Green, Ocean Grey and Medium Sea Grey. The spinner and 18" fuselage band in Sky. Yellow leading edge of the wing. Reddish fabric patches on the machine gun ports. 8" high black serial number obscured by the squadron code and Sky band.

5

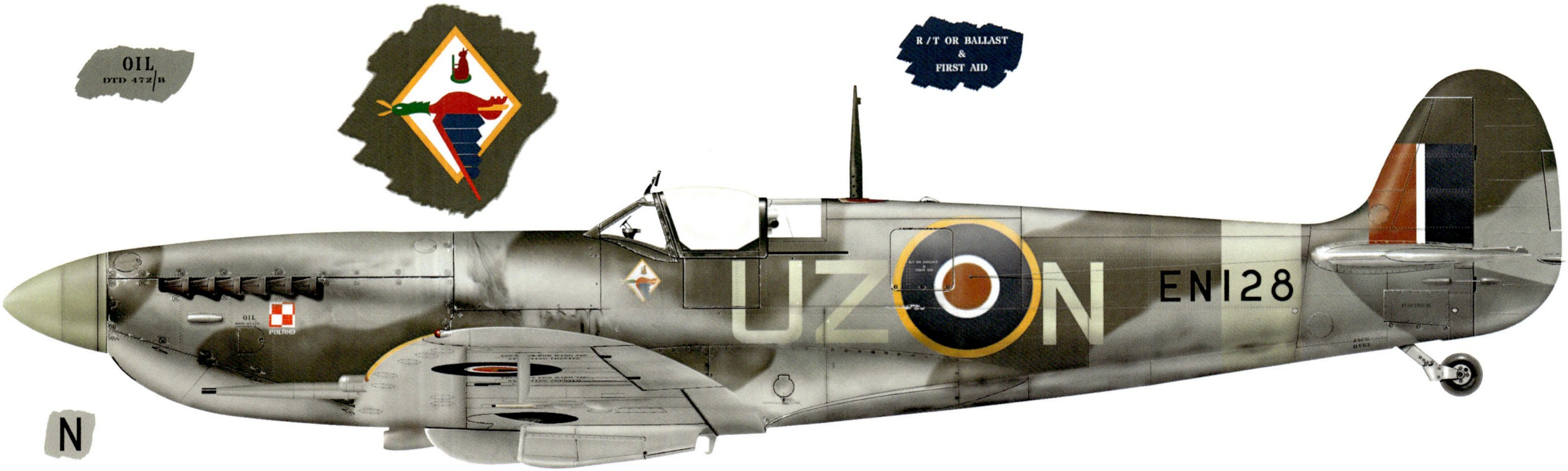

Spitfire F.IX EN128 UZ•N, No. 306 Squadron Polish AF, Northolt, January 1943.

Supermarine-built Spitfire in November 1942, it was delivered to No. 306 Squadron. In January 1943, this aircraft looked heavily worn, with a long area of grey exhaust residue. Standard Day Fighter camouflage, but the fuselage roundel located further forward than usual – note the position of the IFF wire inlet on the red disc of the roundel. The blue background makes the stenciling well visible on the access door to the radio compartment. The N aircraft letter repeated in black below the propeller. No. 306 Squadron badge under the windscreen. An early rectangular rear-view mirror mounted on a taller base as was common on Spitfires in Polish squadrons. This aircraft's armament was limited to two 20mm cannon and two 0.303 in. machine guns. Outer machine guns were removed and their leading edge ports were sealed and overpainted. At that time, this was the standard armament of Spitfire F.IXs in the Polish Wing at Northolt. Note the 30 gal. drop tank under the fuselage. "DTD 472/B" stencilled on above the oil filler access door, to identify the oil standard to be used for the engine.

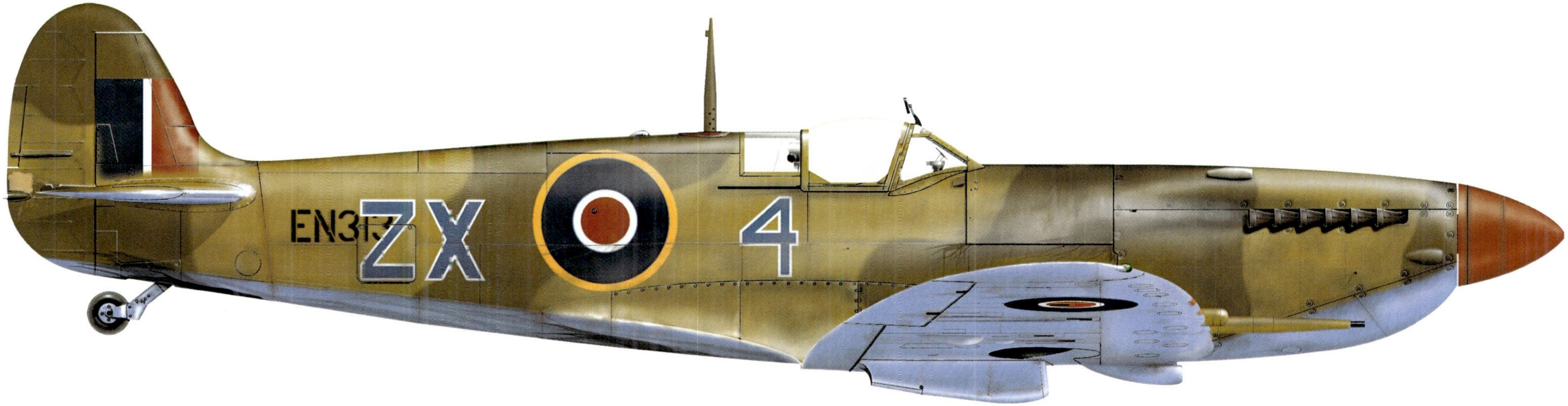

Spitfire F.IX EN313 ZX●4, No 145 Squadron, Polish Combat Team, North Africa, Spring 1943.

This Spitfire used by Polish Combat Team pilots was lucky for F/Lt Wacław Król. He credited with three victories in it: on 4th of April – 1 Bf 109 destroyed, then on 20th of April – 1 MC.202 and finally 1 Bf 109 destroyed next day. The aircraft was in Desert scheme camouflage: Dark Earth and Middle Stone (Midstone) on the upper surfaces and most probably Azure Blue on the bottom. The desert camouflage was sprayed on top of the factory-applied Day Fighter colours. The spinner in Red. The ZX-4 code was most probably in Blue, with white outline. No maintenance stencils were visible on the aircraft, which was not unusual on re-camouflaged aircraft. It is possible that there was a small Polish national marking (white-red chequered square) and victory markings on the port side of the fuel tank cover.

7

Spitfire F.IX EN446 QJ●1, No. 92 Squadron, North Africa, Spring 1943.

This aircraft was delivered to Gibraltar in late February 1943, and allocated to No. 92 Squadron in North Africa soon afterwards. On 20 April 1943 in the morning F/Sgt Michael W. H. Askey flew this Spitfire when he was credited with a Macchi MC.202 destroyed (one of three confirmed victories he scored that day). On 28 April 1943 F/O Thomas W. Savage flew EN446 when he was credited with a Messerschmitt Bf 109 damaged. Both these pilots eventually achieved 'acedom' (Askey with five individual 'kills' and Savage with four individual and one shared), but both were eventually killed while flying with No. 92 Sqn (Savage on 10 July 1943 and Askey on 28 October 1943). The only known photo of the aircraft shows it in the Desert scheme of Dark Earth and Middle Stone on the upper surfaces with the lower surfaces probably in Azure Blue. The spinner was probably black and the aircraft number 1 was white. The QJ squadron code is not certain as the grey shades representing yellow and red are similar in the photograph, but yellow seems more likely.

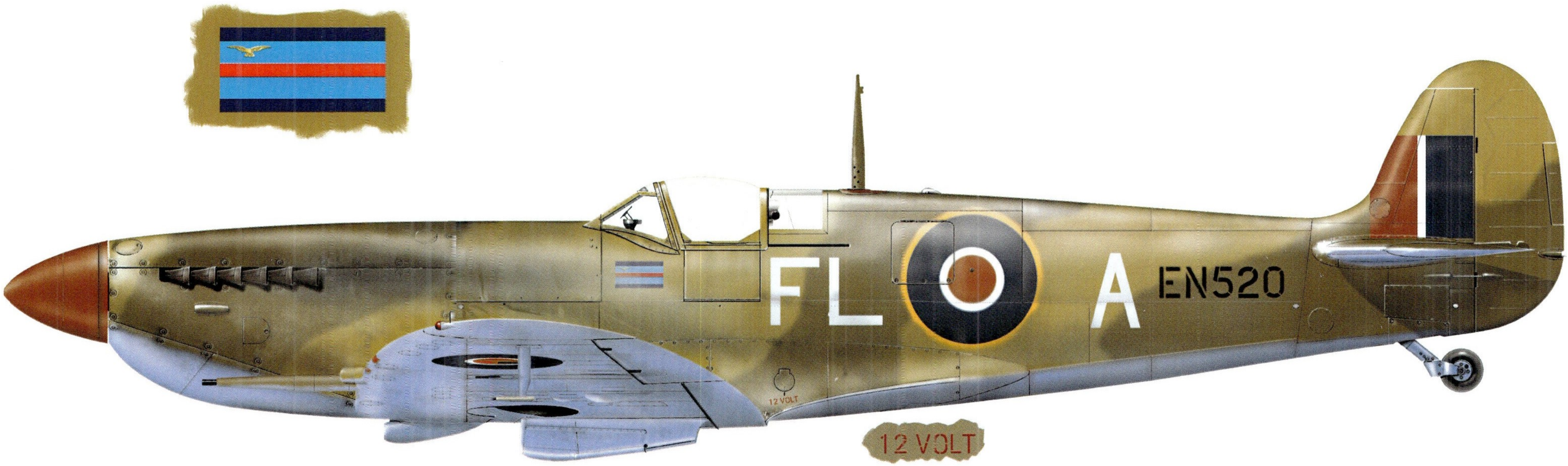

Spitfire F.IX EN520 FL●A, No. 81 Squadron, Souk-el-Khemis, Tunisia, Spring 1943.

Personal mount of S/Ldr Colin Falkland Gray DSO DFC. He was the top scoring New Zealand ace with 27.5 enemy aircraft destroyed to his credit. He was appointed Officer Commanding No. 81 Squadron RAF at the beginning of 1943. This early production Spitfire F.IX was in regular Desert scheme of Dark Earth, Middle Stone and Azure Blue. Red spinner. Code letters seemingly White or Sky. Large Squadron Leader Pennant below windscreen (Air Force Blue with stripes of Dark Blue and Red, and with RAF Eagle in top left corner). The 12 VOLT stencil in Red is visible below the electrical and radio socket. Interestingly, this aircraft, like Gray's other Spitfires, had its rear-view mirror re-fitted inside the windscreen.

9

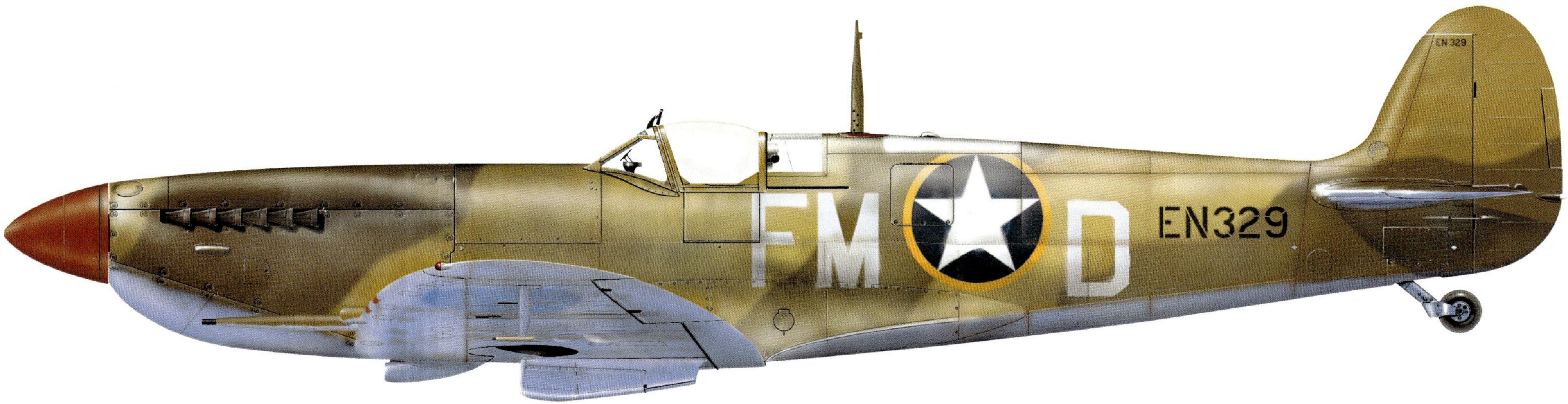

Spitfire F.IX EN329 FM●D, 31st Fighter Group USAAF, Sicily, Summer 1943.

Personal Spitfire of Lt. Col. Fred Murray Dean, Commanding Officer of the 31st Fighter Group 12th Air Force USAAF during the Sicilian campaign. Standard Desert camouflage scheme. Spinner Red or Black. Typical American marking for this period: white star inscribed in the British roundel. The port underwing and starboard upper roundels, as well as the fin flash were overpainted with camouflage. The serial number was stencilled in small size and dark colour at the top of fin. White code letters FM●D: Dean's initials. There is an interesting bright patch above the US national insignia, either unpainted metal or painted white. Note that the white star and code letters were carelessly applied with uneven edges and signs of over spraying.

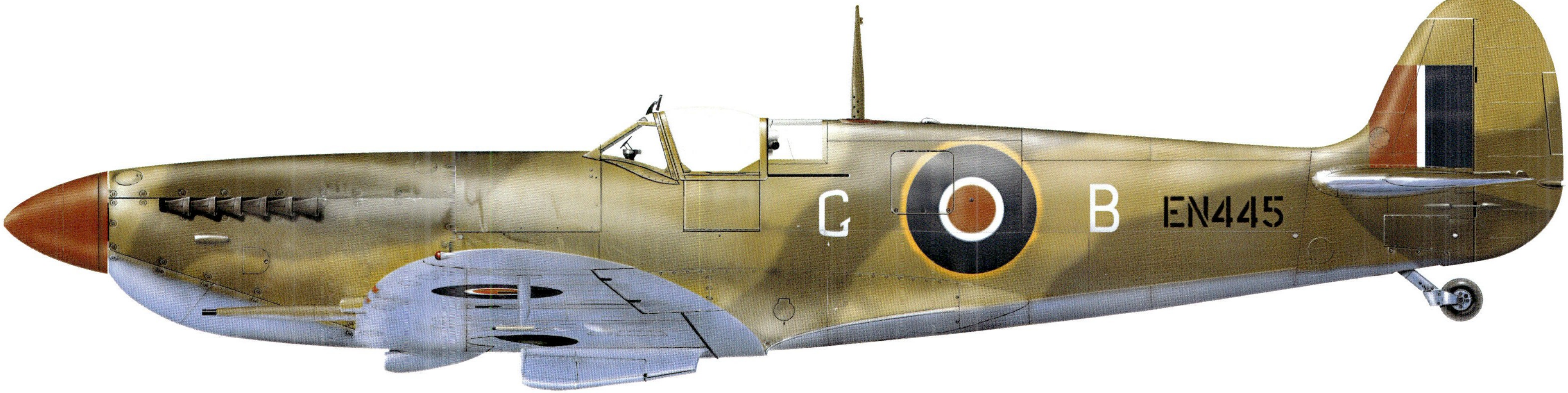

Spitfire F.IX EN445 G●B, No. 81 Squadron RAF, Soukel-Khemis (Paddington), Tunisia, April 1943.

This early Spitfire IX was built by Supermarine in January 1943. For service in North Africa it was re-camouflaged in the Desert colours: Dark Earth, Mid Stone and Azure Blue, with a single-letter squadron code G and aircraft letter B in white. Standard serial number in Black. There were no visible stencils.

11

1.

2.

3.

Spitfire IX QP●N, serial unknown, 2nd Fighter Squadron 52nd Fighter Group USAAF, Summer 1943.

This aircraft was flown during August 1943 by 1Lt Fred Ohr, future American ace. Day Fighter (High Flying) Scheme of Medium Sea Grey on the upper surfaces and PRU Blue underneath. US national markings with red or blue outlines. British fin flash overpainted. Red spinner with a pale (Sky?) back plate. Code letters probably white. No rear-view mirror.

Above standard American national markings on Spitfire IXs: ● White star on a blue disc with yellow border – introduced in October 1942, ●White star on a blue disc with white bars and Insignia Red borders – introduced on 28 June 1943, ●White star on a blue disc with white bars and Insignia Blue borders – from 14 August 1943.

12

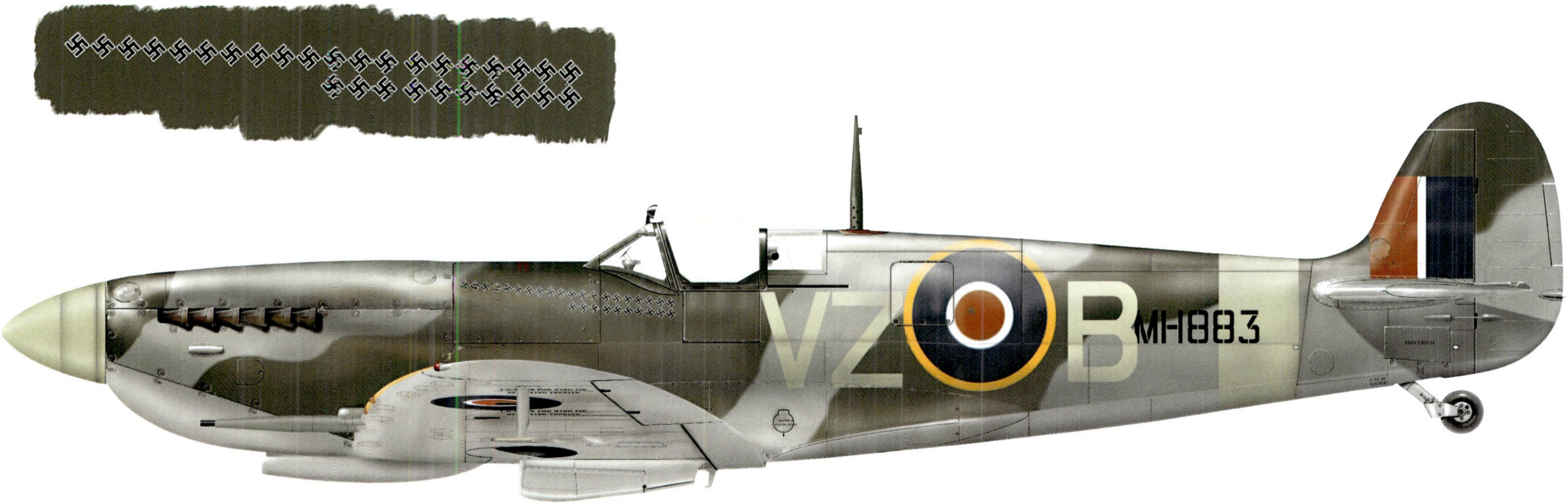

Spitfire LF.IX MH883 VZ●B, No. 412 Squadron RCAF, winter 1943-1944.

This Castle Bromwich built Spitfire during its service with No. 412 Squadron was flown by the Canadian ace George "Buzz"/"Screwball" Beurling DSO DFC DFM. He scored a total of 31 victories during the war, most of these in defence of Malta. This Spitfire is in regular Day Fighter camouflage: Dark Green, Ocean Grey and Medium Sea Grey. The spinner, the band on the fuselage and the code letters were in Sky. His impressive score was painted as 30 swastikas on the port side of the fuel tank cover and below the windscreen.

13

Spitfire F.IX MH353 WX●K "Susan", No. 302 Squadron Polish AF, Northolt, autumn 1943– spring 1944

This Castle Bromwich built Spitfire was transferred to No. 302 Squadron from No. 316 in September 1943. No. 316's code (SZ) was overpainted before the application of the WX. A darker colour patch is visible above the X, in the position of No. 316 Squadron badge. The aircraft letter was retained from the previous squadron but some retouching of the finish is visible near the K. The name "Susan" and No. 302 Squadron badge below the windscreen. A cartoon of a turtle hitting a snail is located on the fuel tank cover, with the caption "WALKA BYKA Z PAROWOZEM" ("A fight between a bull and a steam engine"), presumably meaning a futile effort. White and red stripes applied on cannon firings. Note that there are no outer cannon fittings as a result of Modification 820. Polish national marking below the exhausts. Note the yellow "Y/Y" lubricant class symbols on the oil filler cover. The aircraft letter also applied below the spinner.

Spitfire LF.IX MJ502 OU●L, "PRINCE TUNGI TONGA NO II", No. 485 Squadron RNZAF, early 1944, England.

Unlike the earlier marks, far fewer Spitfire IXs were presentation aircraft with donors' names on the fuselage. MJ502 was the second of three Spitfires founded by the Queen and the people of Tonga. It was delivered to No. 485 Squadron of Royal New Zealand Air Force in January 1944, and usually flown by F/O J.E.P. Yeatman. Standard Day Fighter Scheme with light grey presentation name.

15

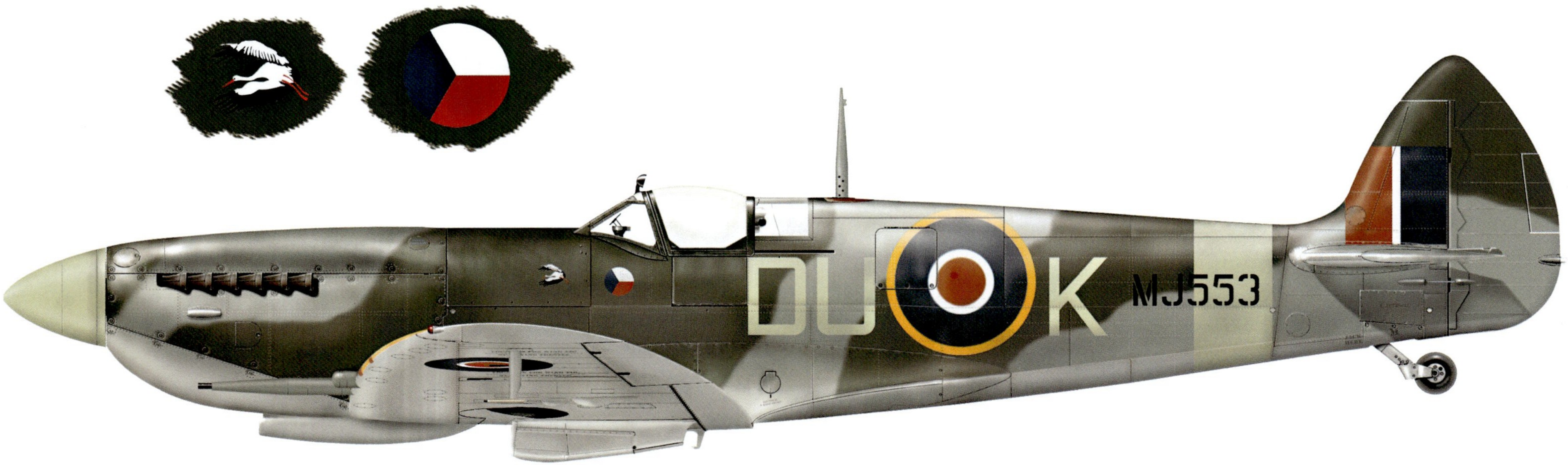

Spitfire LF.IX MJ553 DU●K, No. 312 (Czechoslovak) Squadron RAF, Appledram, April 1944.

The machine was often flown by F/Lt Karel Pošta. Standard camouflage of Dark Green, Ocean Grey and Medium Sea Grey. Sky spinner and fuselage band. The Czechoslovak national marking was applied below the windscreen. The flying stork painted on the fuel tank cover was an official No. 312 Squadron badge. Note the broad chord rudder. Later, this aeroplane was converted to the FR.IX version and was used by No. 414 Squadron RCAF.

Spitfire IX EP●A, England 1944.

Personal aircraft of Lt Col. Emmette F. Allen, 9th Tactical Air Command. The black EP●A code was his personal marking. Polished natural metal finish overall, but the rudder remained in original camouflage. There is an narrow anti-glare panel in front of the windscreen, probably in Olive Drab. The spinner was probably in Sky. There was no patch on the signal discharger port. The late IFF system antenna under the wing. Note the Rebbeca beam approach system with its antenna below the fuselage.

Spitfire F.IX MA425 RZ●R, No. 241 Squadron RAF, Italy, January 1944.

This Spitfire, built at the CBAF in July 1943, finished its career on 4 October 1944. It is in Day Fighter scheme, still has the Sky fuselage band, but the Spinner colour was changed to Black. Interestingly, there is no yellow leading edge stripe. Red codes. Different shape of letters R attract attention. Note the repair marks visible on the rudder.

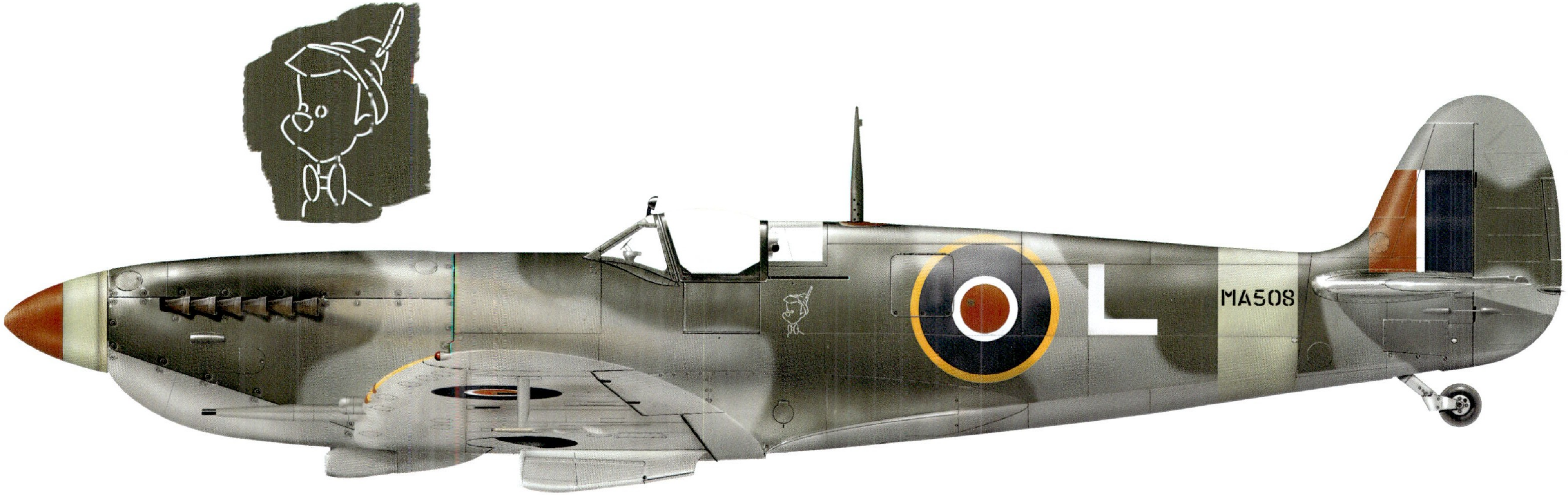

Spitfire F.IX MA508 L, No. 10 Squadron SAAF, Idku, Egypt, Summer 1944.

Built in June 1943 with Merlin 63 engine. Flown by Lt George Segella. The aircraft seems to have been repainted in the Day Fighter scheme (B pattern) with Sky fuselage band and a small size serial number. Aircraft letter L probably white. Two-tone spinner, probably in Sky with a Red front section. The Pinocchio motif painted aft of the cockpit door probably dated from No. 94 Squadron RAF, where the machine was used previously. The Aboukir air filter on the carburettor air intake is of interest.

19

Spitfire F.IX MA565 WR●G, No. 40 Squadron SAAF, Italy, 1944.

The machine is painted Aluminium (silver colour) overall with a dark anti-glare panel. Squadron letters in white. The spinner was dark, probably Red. The red in roundels and fin flash was replaced with orange, as was often seen in South African Air Force squadrons. DTD 63A C symbols stencilled above the fin flash suggest cellulose enamel with glossy finish applied on the airplane.

Spitfire LF.IX JL132 WU•X, No. 225 Squadron RAF, Corsica, July 1944.

Built as a Spitfire VC, it was converted to Spitfire IX with Rolls-Royce Merlin 66 (LF standard). It was lost on operations, when flown by F/O Peter G. Cable on 27 August 1944. Freshly applied Day Fighter colours in B pattern. Code letters probably Yellow with small personal marking "JP" – possibly for F/Lt J. Pratt, probably in Sky. Red spinner. Small serial number. Note the anti-glare fences fitted on the fuel tank cover, very rarely seen on Spitfires.

Spitfire LF.IX JL172 (most probably A), No. 73 Squadron RAF, Italy 1944.

Built as a Spitfire VC and converted to Spitfire LF.IX with Merlin 66. It was used by 73 Squadron from August until it was lost in November 1944. Single-tone camouflage, which could be Medium Sea Grey. The serial number was left from a previous colour scheme, with a window of a different colour (Middle Stone?) around it. No. 73 squadron's geometrical emblem with unknown colours. Other pictures of 73 Sqn Spitfires IX (EN199 W, SM147 Z, MJ238 X) suggest the main colour of the emblem was darker than Roundel Blue and the narrow stripes were neither Yellow, Red, nor White.

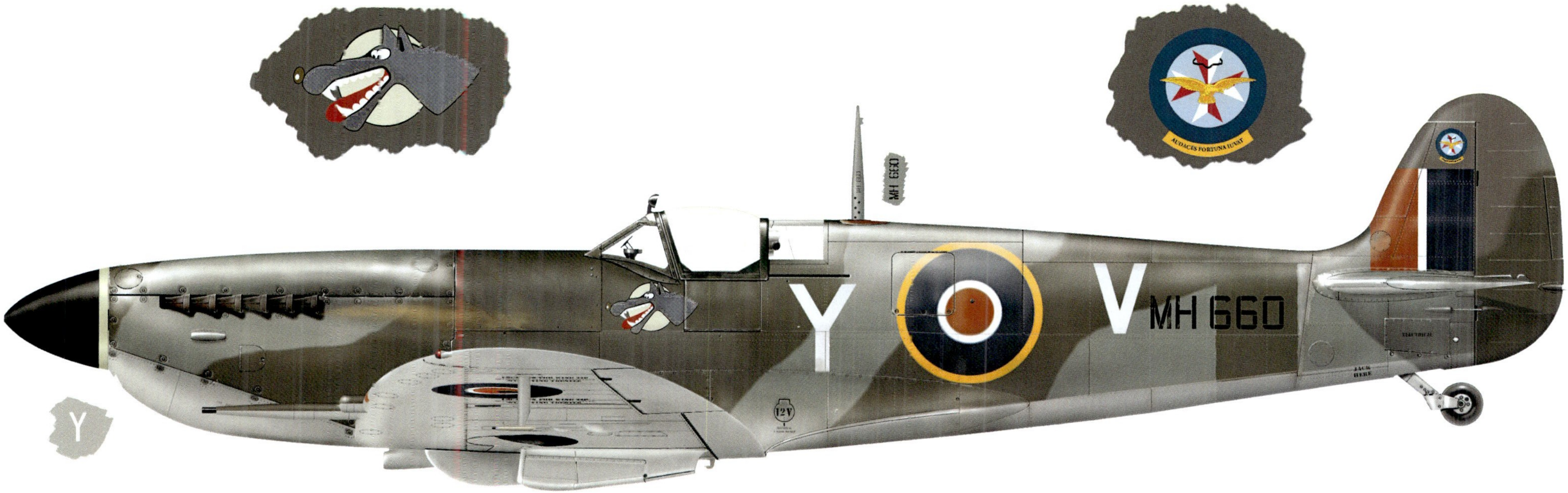

Spitfire F.IX MH660 Y•V, No. 1435 Squadron RAF, Italy, mid-1944.

Built in September 1943 at the CBAF, it served with No. 1435 Squadron mostly as a fighter-bomber within the Balkan Air Forces. The aircraft was delivered in the Day Fighter Scheme, but Sky band on the fuselage was later overpainted. The Sky spinner was repainted Black rather than Red and the back plate was left in Sky. No. 1435 Squadron single-letter code V and the aircraft letter Y were white. A small Y was applied below the propeller. The "Wolf and moon" cartoon under the windscreen may be related to the previous night fighter role of the squadron at Malta. No. 1435 Squadron badge was at the top of the fin. The rudder and a fin seem repainted with the colours transposed. Note the serial number on the antenna mast. A 30 gallon slipper tank is attached under the fuselage.

Spitfire F.IX MH946 No. 10 Squadron SAAF, Idku, Egypt 1944.

The Spitfire was converted to intercept enemy aircraft at very high altitudes. To improve high-altitude performance, pointed wingtips were added, the radio equipment and mast were removed, the armament was reduced to two .303 inch guns in cannon bays. No camouflage or national markings. Only a small serial number for identification. The fabric covered rudder and the elevator were painted silver colour. Similarly converted Spitfires were used by No. 41 Squadron SAAF at Lakatamia, Cyprus and called "S.H.F Spitfires". There was a special interception tactics for two of these modified Spitfires differing with armament. The lighter one, armed with machine guns only, attacked the high-flying enemy to force them down, where the heavier armed Spitfire with cannon could finish off the attack.

Spitfire LF.IXe PT530 FT●A, No. 43 Squadron RAF, August 1944.

This Spitfire was flown by S/Ldr Arthur H. Jupp during operations in Southern Europe. The main role of No. 43 Squadron at the time was ground attack, and the machine carries a 250lb MP bomb attached to the Mk III Universal bomb carrier under the fuselage. The Day Fighter Scheme features a precisely overpainted Sky band with the serial number re-applied. Red spinner with the back plate left in Sky. Code letters probably Black with white outline. Late broad chord rudder.

Spitfire LF.IX MK210, Bluie West, Greenland, June 1944.

This Spitfire was tested in the USA to check the possibility of increasing its operational range. After the tests it was flown to Britain across the Atlantic by Lt. Col. Gustav Lundquist, the Chief Experimental Fighter Test Pilot. During a stop on Greenland, Sergeant Petta created the unique colourful nose art. Tolly was Lundquist's wife's name. For this flight the aircraft was modified by adding an additional fuel tank behind the cockpit and large external underwing tanks. Factory-applied Day Fighter camouflage with standard markings. Note the fuel filler behind cockpit. No gunsight.

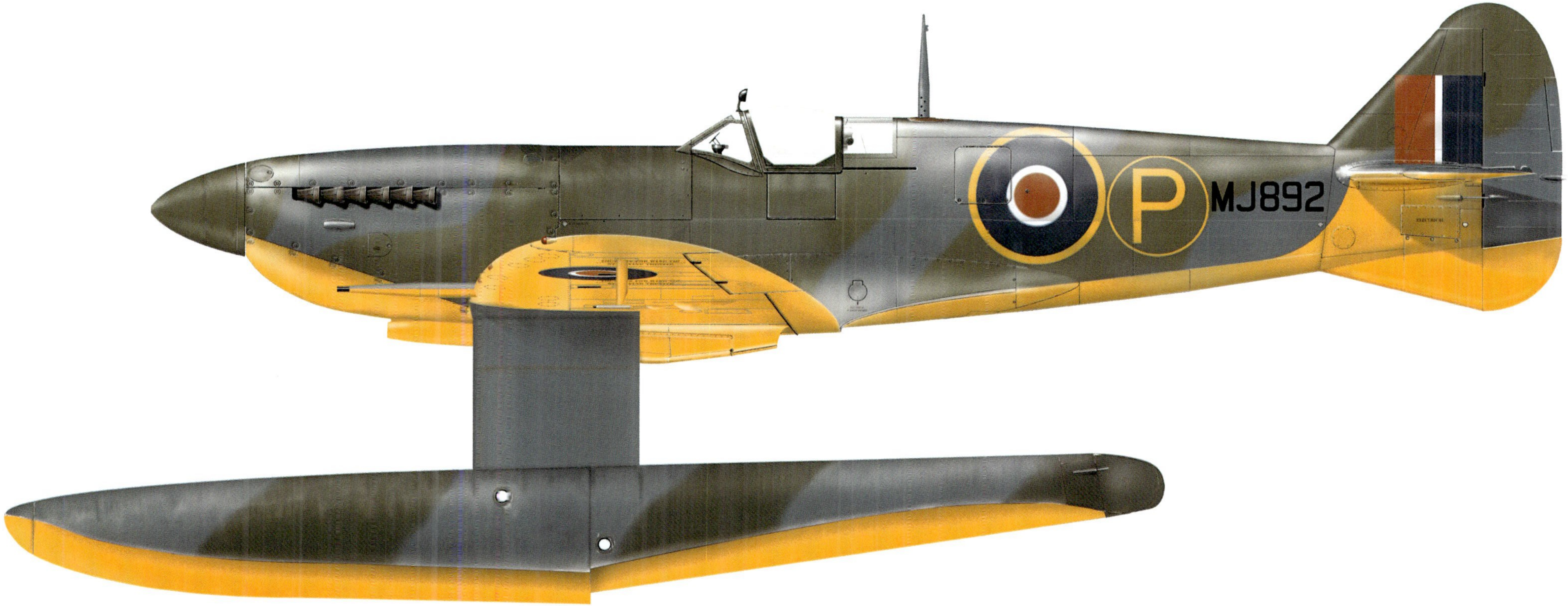

Spitfire IX MJ892, June 1944.

Built as a Spitfire LF.IX, it was delivered to Rotols, Staverton on December 1943 to be converted to Type 385 floatplane with first flight in June 1944. Upper surfaces were camouflaged in the Temperate Sea Scheme of Extra Dark Sea Grey and Dark Slate Grey. The underside was Yellow. Yellow ring with letter P was a marking of experimental aircraft. Outer cannon ports were removed.

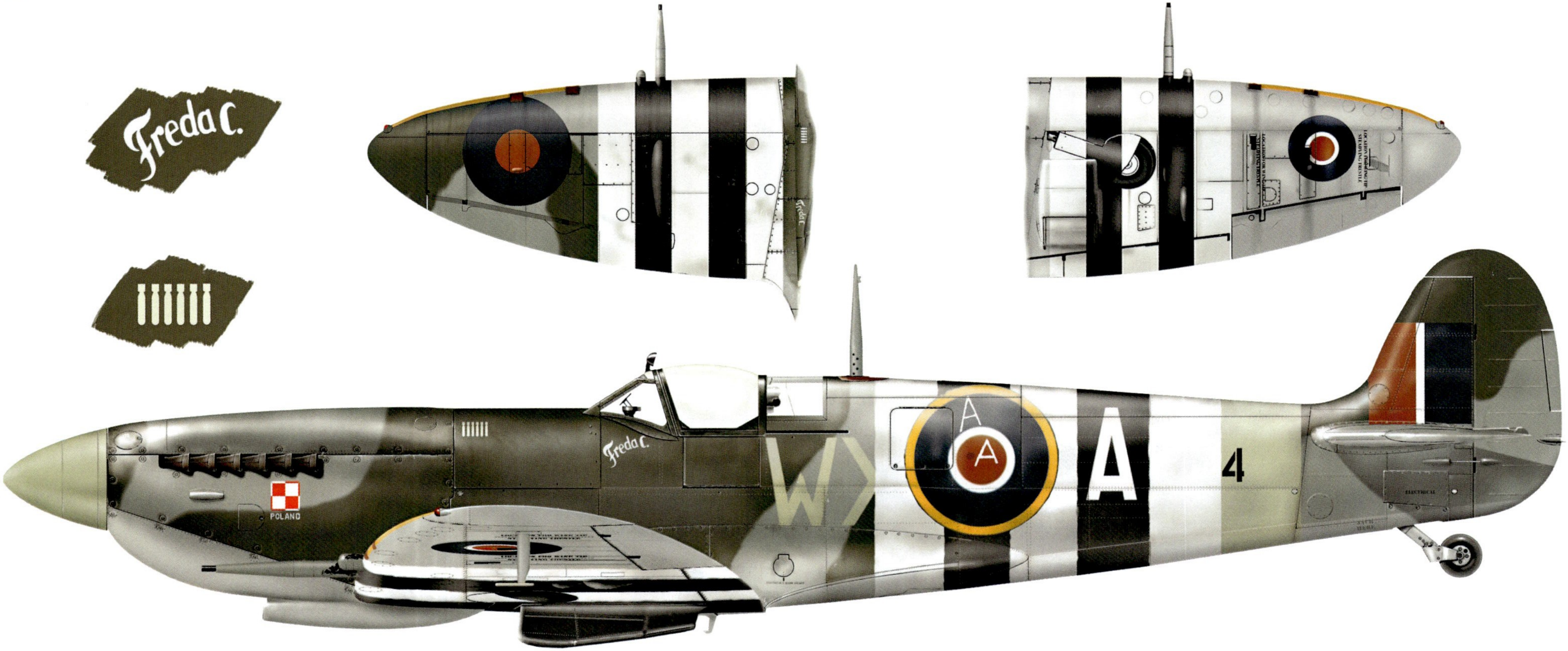

Spitfire LF.IX MK924 WX●A, "Freda C." No. 302 Squadron Polish AF, Chailey, June 1944.

This Spitfire was flown by F/Sgt Michał Murayda, a Polish volunteer from the USA. The Day Fighter scheme was covered with full D-Day markings on the fuselage and wings: black and white stripes 18" wide, which obscured the aircraft letter as well as a part of the squadron code and the serial number. The aircraft letter a was reapplied in three (!) locations on fuselage. The letters on the roundel were probably chalked on temporarily. The personal name "Freda C." was probably White. Six bomb mission symbols on the fuel tank cover possibly in Sky.

Spitfire LF.IX MJ586 LO●D, No. 602 Squadron RAF, summer 1944.

This machine was flown by the French ace Pierre Clostermann. On 29 June 1944, he claimed a FW 190 shot down while flying this Spitfire. Next day he scored an Bf 109 probably destroyed. His victory markings are visible below the windscreen. The machine is in the Day Fighter scheme with worn out D-Day stripes. The badge below the exhausts is that of No. 602 "City of Glasgow" Squadron: red lion of Scotland on a white shield.

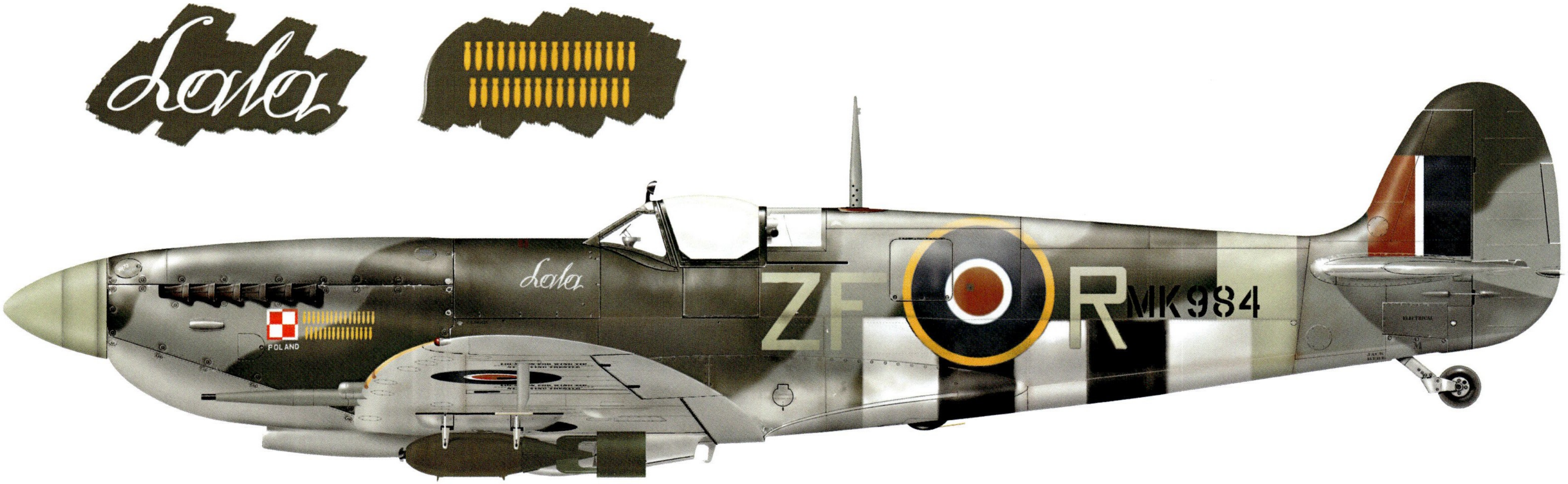

Spitfire LF.IX MK984 ZF●R “Lala”, No. 308 Squadron Polish AF, autumn 1944.

This Spitfire was usually flown by S/Ldr Witold Retinger. The personal name “Lala” (Doll) referred to his girlfriend. Day Fighter scheme with D-Day stripes only on the lower part of the fuselage. 31 yelow bomb mission symbols just aft of the Polish national marking. Note the camouflage colour division line kink between the upper and port engine cowling panels. This aircraft was equipped with the Rebecca beam approach system with the antenna on the bottom of the fuselage. Factory-applied stencils are visible on the starboard side of the rudder, including “DTD 308 C” for the cellulose lacquer on the canvas covered rudder and “DTD 314 S” for the synthetic lacquer on the metal fin covering. The late type IFF aerial is under the starboard wing. 250lb Medium Capacity bombs are attached under wings.

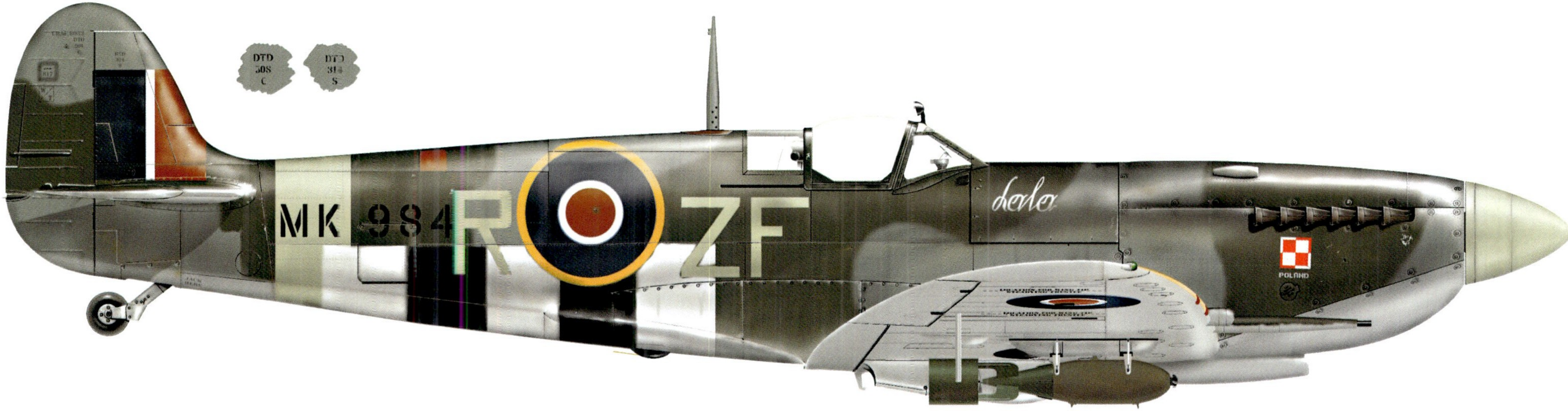

Spitfire LF.IX MK984 ZF●R “Lala”, No 308 Squadron PAF, autumn 1944.

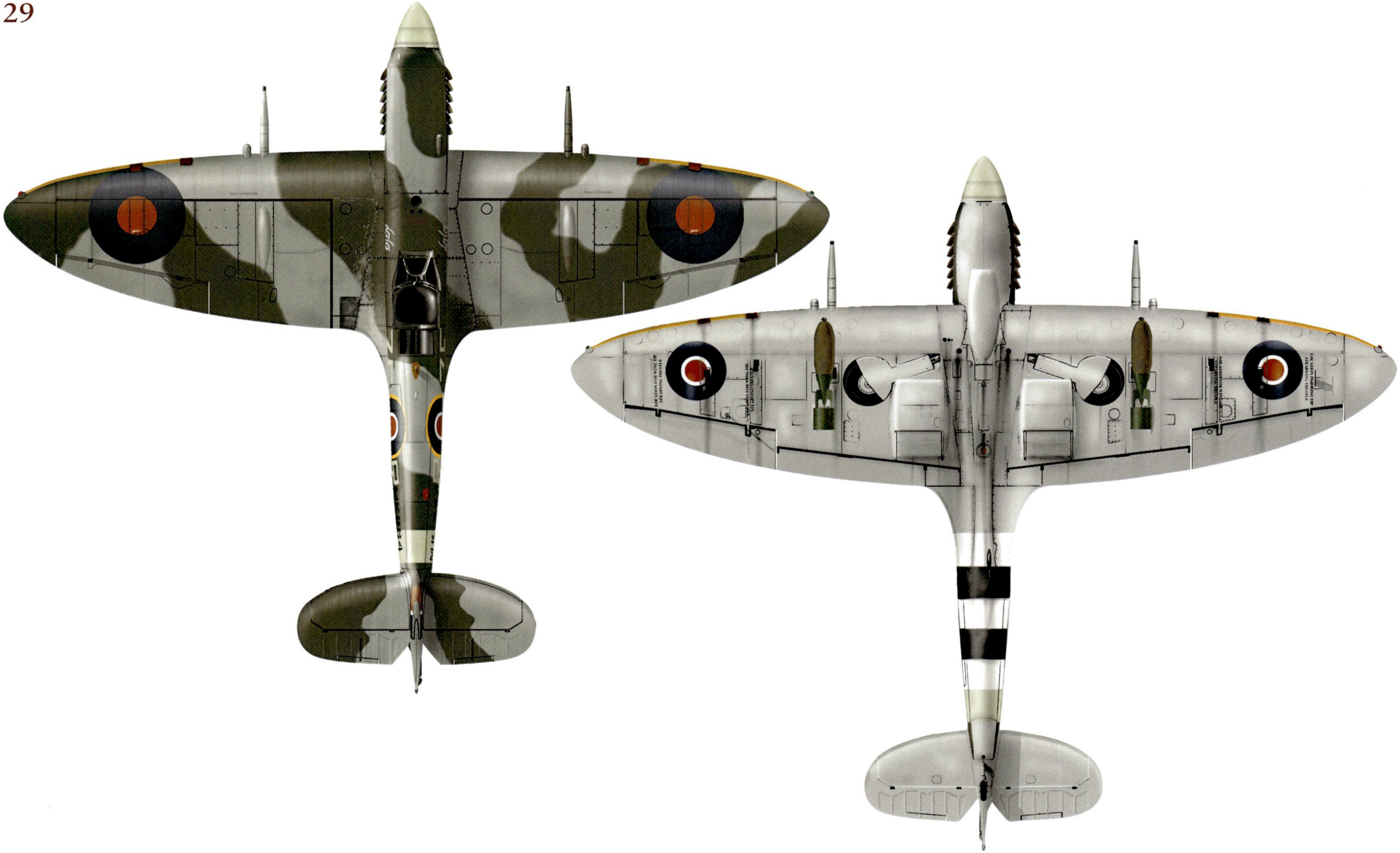

Spitfire LF.IX MK984 ZF●R "Lala", No 308 Squadron PAF, autumn 1944.

Spitfire FR.IX MK716 X, No. 16 Squadron RAF, September 1944, Bayeux, France.

Built as an LF.IX and later modified for fighter reconnaissance: FR. Rarely seen PRU Pink camouflage overall. Two-tone (blue and red) roundels on the fuselage and upper wing surface, but three-tone small 12" fin flashes. D-Day stripes only on the lower part of the fuselage, and traces of invasion stripes still visible on the wings undersides. Aircraft letter X most probably in Red. Small serial number stencilled above fin flash in Blue.

Spitfire LF.IX MH712 WX●D "Pat", No. 302 Squadron Polish AF, autumn 1944.

The aeroplane was usually flown by W/O Henryk Dygała. Day Fighter camouflage scheme. Personal badge: a girl sitting on a bomb and the name Pat on the side of the engine cowling. Invasion stripes on the underside of the fuselage and under the wings. Small, ca. 2 in. tall, serial number located at the top of the fin. Yellow inscription "WYCIERAĆ OBUWIE" (Wipe your shoes) aft of the cockpit door. Note the white markings of the fasteners position on the tail wheel cover. White stencils on the inspection door of the radio compartment: W/T OR BALLAST instead of R/T OR BALLAST. It looks like the rudder was repainted because the camouflage colours have sharp edges, unlike those on the fuselage. Small aircraft letter applied under the propeller spinner in black. A dark, probably rusty, patch is applied on the red disc of fuselage roundel to seal the old IFF system antenna port. The machine carries two MC 250 lb bombs on the underwing carriers and one MC 500 lb bomb with short tail unit (No. 28) under the fuselage.

Spitfire LF.IX MK805 SH•B "Peter John III", No. 64 Squadron RAF, autumn 1944.

F/Lt Tony Cooper flew this Spitfire seventy one times. Peter John were the names of his son. Day Fighter scheme with incorrect invasion markings. In No. 64 Squadron the stripes on the fuselage and wings were much narrower than required. Aircraft letter B was painted on the rudder. The serial number is reapplied on the Sky band with smaller characters, and traces of the previous, regular size serial number can be seen below. A 90-gallon slipper tank is attached under the fuselage. This Spitfire survived the war and today it can be seen at the Museo Storico dell'Aeronautica Militare at Vigna di Valle, Italy.

33

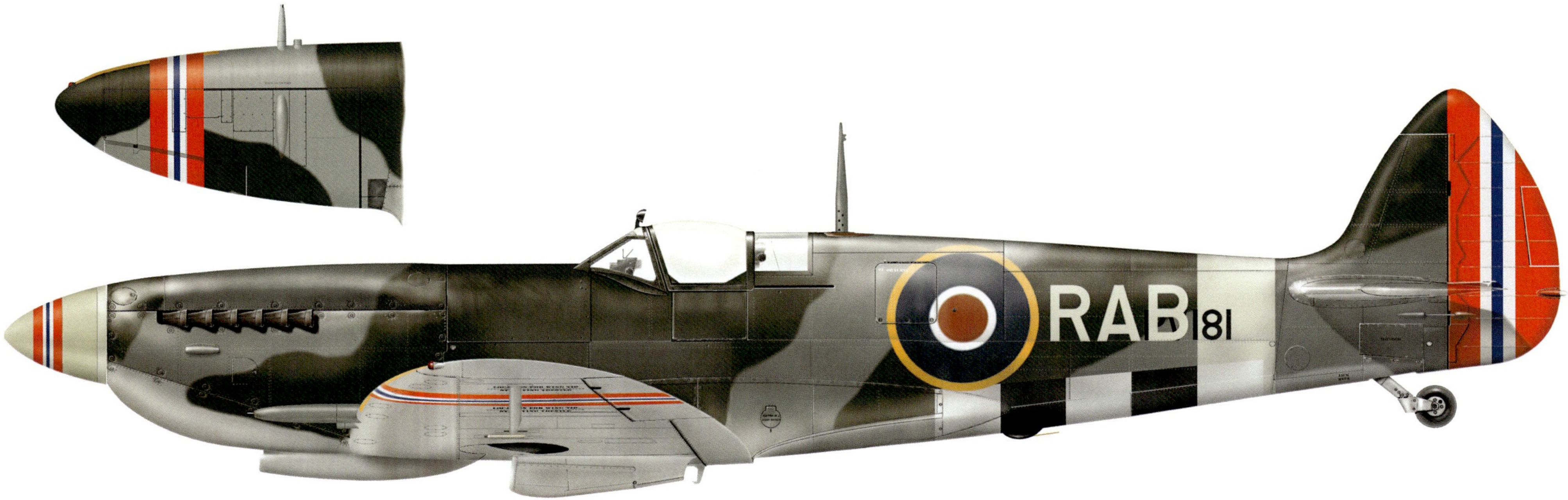

Spitfire LF.IXe PV181 RAB, No. 132 (Norwegian) Wing, autumn 1944.

The Spitfire was usually flown by the Norwegian ace W/Cdr Rolf Arne Berg DFC. In October–November 1944 he requested to apply the pre-war style Norwegian markings on his personal Spitfire. His plan to mark in a similar way all the Norwegian Spitfires in No. 132 Wing was not approved by higher echelons and the Spitfire was repainted before end of 1944. Note the Rebecca beam approach system with the antenna below the fuselage and the late Gyro Sight Mk II in the cockpit.

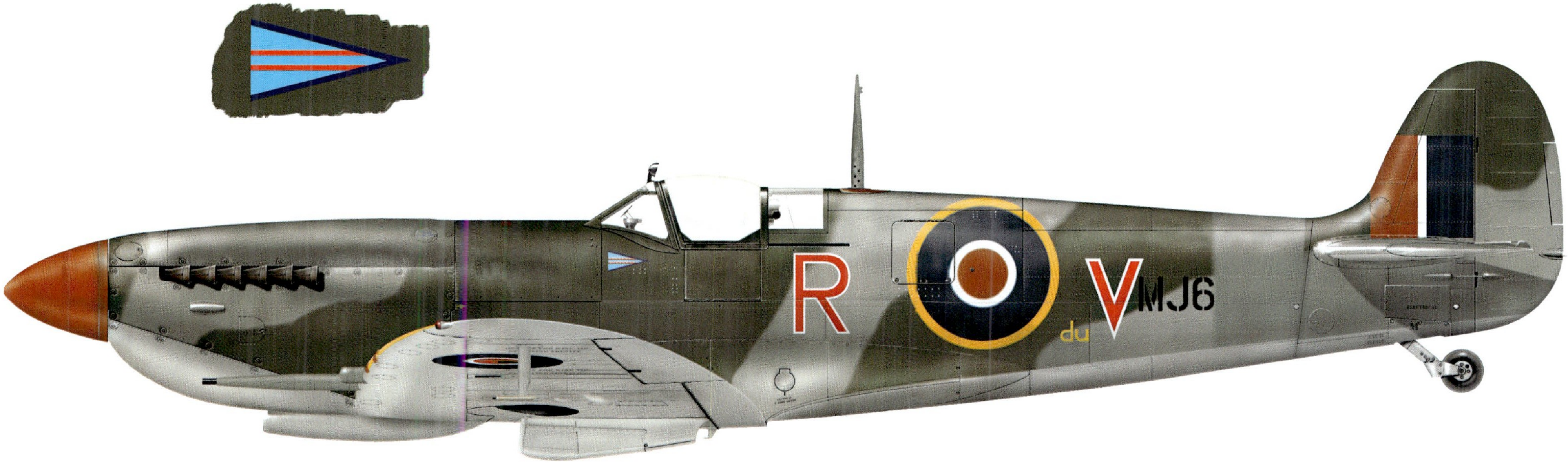

Spitfire LF.IX MJ625 R●duV, No. 239 Wing RAF, Tarquinia, Italy, June 1944.

The personal mount of W/Cdr Raymond du Vivier, Commanding No. 239 Wing RAF. Day Fighter Scheme with the Sky band and a part of the serial number overpainted. "R du V" was the personal marking of the pilot. The letters R and V were probably Red and "du" was Yellow. The spinner was repainted Red. A Wing Commander pennant was applied below the windscreen.

Spitfire HF.IXe PL458 WR●T.C. "Orissa IX", No. 40 Squadron SAAF, Italy 1944/1945.

Built as an HF version with a Merlin 70 engine, it was delivered to No. 40 Squadron. Coded T.C. for its pilot, Capt. Trevor Cook. Repainted in the Day Fighter scheme with a non-standard pattern. National markings with red colour replaced by orange. Orange spinner with a brighter (Sky) back plate. Black serial number applied with a smaller size stencil. Clipped wingtips. The inboard 0.5 inch machine gun fairings have been removed, but the armament seems to have been retained, as the fabric patches are visible there. A large squadron badge on the engine cover.

Spitfire LF.IX MJ478 8J•GG, No. 326 (French) Squadron RAF (GC II/7 "Nice"), Italy, early 1945.

Flown by French ace Lt Gabriel Gauthier. Standard Day Fighter scheme of Dark Green, Ocean Grey and Medium Sea Grey, with overpainted Sky band and fin flash. Highly modified national markings: British roundel changed to French colours and proportions, the British fin flash deleted and a French "tricolore" painted on the rudder. The squadron and personal letters were probably in Sky or white.

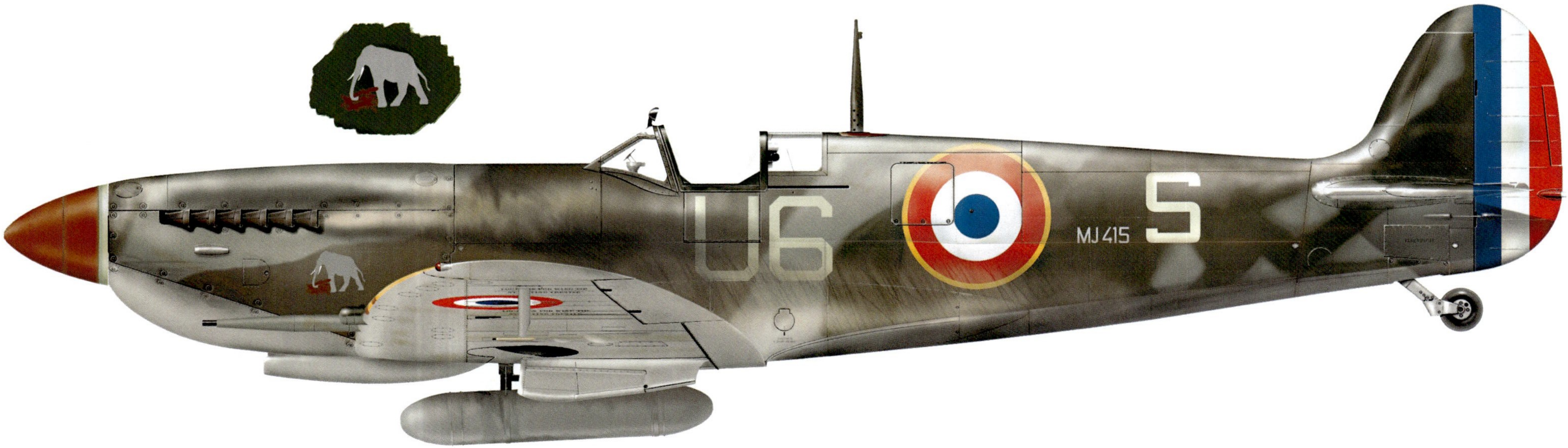

Spitfire LF.IX MJ415 U6●S, No. 327 (French) Squadron RAF (GC I/3 "Corse"), 1945.

Another French Spitfire. The tail was overpainted in a random manner to obliterate the Sky band and the British fin flash. The rudder was painted in the French colours. The serial number applied in small size just aft of the fuselage roundel, possibly in Medium Sea Grey. Code letters in Sky. Red spinner with the back plate in Sky. Note the personal badge on the cowling: an elephant with logs. Note the 50 gallon torpedo fuel tank on Mk.III bomb carrier under the fuselage.

Spitfire LF.IX MK392 JE●J, 127 Wing, B.56 Evere, Belgium, January 1945.

Personal aircraft of W/Cdr James Edgar "Johnnie" Johnson CB, CBE, DSO & Two Bars, DFC & Bar, DL. This British ace was credited with 34 individual victories. The aircraft is in typical Day Fighter scheme with the early 1945 markings: Sky band was obliterated, the spinner overpainted black. The underwing roundels had yellow outer rings and the roundels on upper wing surfaces were in four tones of red, white, blue and yellow.

Spitfire LF.IXe PT959 CFB, "JOAN TOO", No. 132 (Norwegian) Wing, April 1945, Twente/Enschede, Nederlands.

Personal Spitfire of G/Cpt C.F. Bradley, Commanding No. 132 Wing. The personalised small size codes in white. Note that the entire fuselage aft of roundel was repainted. A very small serial number was applied on a window left of the overpainted Sky band. "JOAN TOO" was a name applied after Bradley's wife. A Wing Commander pennant was applied below the windscreen. The spinner was painted white and black or blue. Typically for that time, the wing roundels were red/white/blue/yellow.

Spitfire UTI, USSR, Early 1945.

A Spitfire IX modified in the USSR into a two-seat trainer. The front cockpit remained in its original position. The armament was removed. Note the older, HF wire type antenna between the fuselage and rudder, typical for Spitfires delivered to the USSR. All surfaces finished in a dark colour, probably green.

Published in Poland in 2023
by STRATUS sp.j.
ul. Żeromskiego 6A, 27-600 Sandomierz, Poland
e-mail: office@mmpbooks.biz
as
MMPBooks

ISBN
978-83-67227-41-4

Editor in chief
Roger Wallsgrove

Editorial Team
Bartłomiej Belcarz
Robert Pęczkowski
Artur Juszczak

Colour profiles
Robert Grudzień

DTP
Stratus sp.j.

Printed by
Partner Poligrafia
ul. Szosa Baranowicka 77
15-523 Białystok
Grabówka

PRINTED IN POLAND

Selected Bibliography

Belcarz, B., Gretzyngier, R., Kopański, T. J., Matusiak, W., Rogusz, M., Zmyślony, W., *Polish Fighter Colours 1939-1947 vol.2*, MMP Books 2021.
Boot, Henry, Sturtivant, Ray, *Gifts of War*, An Air-Britain Publication 2005.
Bracken, Robert, *Spitfire. The Canadians*, Boston Mill Press 1995.
Dunstan, John, Rawlings, Richard, *Fighter Squadrons of the R.A.F. and Their Aircraft*, Crecy, 1992.
Hurt, Zdeněk, *Naši se vraceji*, Eduard 2017.
Laird, Malcolm, Mackenzie, Steve, *Spitfire The ANZACS The RAF through Colonial eyes*, Ventura Publications 1997.
Ludwig, Paul, Laird, Malcolm, *American Spitfire Camouflage And Markings*, Ventura Publications 1998.
Matusiak, Wojtek, *Supermarine Spitfire IX 1942-1943*, Polish Wings 13, Stratus 2011.
Matusiak, Wojtek, *Supermarine Spitfire IX 1944-1946*, Polish Wings 15, Stratus 2012.
Matusiak, Wojtek, *Supermarine Spitfire vol. 3*, Monografie Lotnicze, AJ Press 1999.
Matusiak, Wojtek, *Supermarine Spitfire vol.4*, Monografie Lotnicze, AJ Press 2000.
McLean, Steven, *The Spitfire in South African Air Force Service*, GR Printing Publishing 2001.
Morgan, Eric B., Shacklady, Edward, *Spitfire The History*, Key Publishing 1987.
Moss, Peter, Bachelor, Len, *Supermarine Spitfire Mk. IX*, Profile 206, Profile Publication Ltd. London.
Price, Alfred, *Spitfire. A Complete Fighting History*, PRC Ltd 1992.
Price, Alfred, *Supermarine Spitfire vol.1*, Monografie Lotnicze, AJ Press 1997.
Terbeck, Helmut, van der Meer, Harry, Sturtivant, Ray, *Spitfire International*, Air Britain Publication 2002.
Thomas, Andrew, *American Spitfire Aces of World War 2*, Osprey Publishing 2007.

Other sources:
Wojtek Matusiak archive
Imperial War Museum archive
www.norwegianspitfire.com